W9-AJT-336

JAN 3 0 2008

GREENACRES BRANCH
LIBRARY

DISCARDED

J 623 .82 LIN
Lindeen, Mary.
Ships /

**PALM BEACH COUNTY
LIBRARY SYSTEM**
3650 Summit Boulevard
West Palm Beach, FL 33406-4198

Ships

by Mary Lindeen

BELLWETHER MEDIA • MINNEAPOLIS, MN

Note to Librarians, Teachers, and Parents:

Blastoff! Readers are carefully developed by literacy experts and combine standards-based content with developmentally appropriate text.

Level 1 provides the most support through repetition of high-frequency words, light text, predictable sentence patterns, and strong visual support.

Level 2 offers early readers a bit more challenge through varied simple sentences, increased text load, and less repetition of high-frequency words.

Level 3 advances early-fluent readers toward fluency through increased text and concept load, less reliance on visuals, longer sentences, and more literary language.

Whichever book is right for your reader, Blastoff! Readers are the perfect books to build confidence and encourage a love of reading that will last a lifetime!

This edition first published in 2007 by Bellwether Media.

No part of this publication may be reproduced in whole or in part without written permission of the publisher. For information regarding permission, write to Bellwether Media Inc., Attention: Permissions Department, Post Office Box 1C, Minnetonka, MN 55345-9998.

Library of Congress Cataloging-in-Publication Data
Lindeen, Mary.
  Ships / by Mary Lindeen.
    p. cm. — (Blastoff! Readers) (Mighty machines)
Summary: "Simple text and supportive full-color photographs introduce young readers to ships. Intended for kindergarten through third grade"—Provided by publisher.
  Includes bibliographical references and index.
  ISBN-13: 978-1-60014-060-0 (hardcover : alk. paper)
  ISBN-10: 1-60014-060-2 (hardcover : alk. paper)
  1. Ships—Juvenile literature. I. Title.

VM150.L494 2007
623.82'04—dc22   2006035262

Text copyright © 2007 by Bellwether Media.
SCHOLASTIC, CHILDREN'S PRESS, and associated logos are trademarks and/or registered trademarks of Scholastic Inc.
Printed in the United States of America.

Contents

A ship is
a big boat.
It travels on
the ocean.

A ship has
a **captain**.
The captain
is in charge.

A ship has
a **deck**.
People sit
and stand
on the deck.

A ship has an **engine**. Some ship engines fill a whole room.

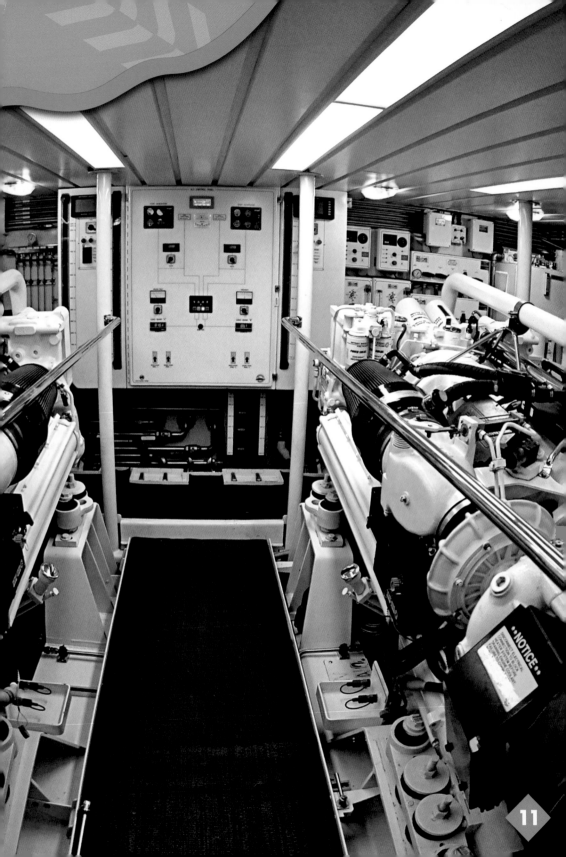

An engine makes this **cargo** ship move. A cargo ship carries **goods** across the ocean.

This tall ship has **sails**. The wind pushes the sails and makes the ship move.

This
supertanker
carries oil.

This aircraft carrier carries airplanes.

This **cruise** ship carries people on a trip. Have fun!

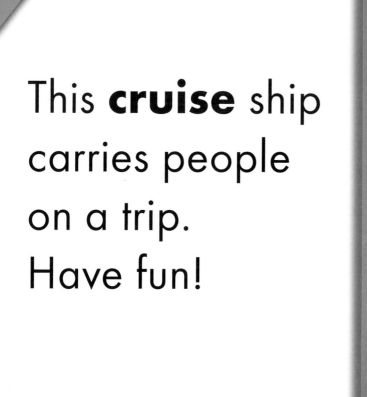

Glossary

captain—the person in charge of a ship and its crew

cargo—freight that is carried by an airplane, ship, or truck

cruise—a vacation on a ship that stops at several different places

deck—the floor on the top level of a ship

engine—a machine that uses fuel to move

goods—items that are bought and sold

sails—the sheets of fabric that hang above a ship and catch the wind

supertanker—a very big tanker ship that carries oil

To Learn More

AT THE LIBRARY

Armentrout, David and Patricia Armentrout. *Ships*. Vero Beach, FL: Rourke, 2003.

Haslam, Andrew and Andrew Solway. *Ships*. Minnetonka, MN: Two-Can, 2000.

Pipe, Jim. *How Does a Ship Float*? East Grinstead, UK: Copper Beech, 2002.

ON THE WEB

Learning more about mighty machines is as easy as 1, 2, 3.

1. Go to www.factsurfer.com

2. Enter "mighty machines" into search box.

3. Click the "Surf" button and you will see a list of related web sites.

With factsurfer.com, finding more information is just a click away.

Index

The photographs in this book are reproduced through the courtesy of: Ian Klein, front cover; Gertjan Hooljer, p. 5; Gavin Hellier/Alamy, p. 7; Blaz Kure, p. 9; Albert Barr, p. 11; Lester Lefkowitz/Getty Images, p. 13; Marco van Belleghem, p. 15; Martin Rogers/Getty Images, p. 17; Lisa Marcus/Courtesy of the US Navy/Getty Images, p. 19; David Hecker/AFP/Getty Images, p. 21.